British Glamour
since 1950

BALLGOWNS

BALLG

V&A Publishing

British Glamour
since 1950

OWNS

Oriole Cullen
Sonnet Stanfill

Photographs by David Hughes

Learning Resources
Centre

13892703

First published by V&A Publishing,
2012
V&A Publishing
Victoria and Albert Museum
South Kensington
London SW7 2RL
www.vandabooks.com

Distributed in North America by
Harry N. Abrams, Inc., New York

Hardback edition
ISBN 9781 85177 684 9

Library of Congress Control
Number 2011935135

10 9 8 7 6 5 4 3 2
2015 2014 2013 2012

Designer: Adam Brown_01.02
Copy Editor: Denny Hemming

Printed in Italy

MIX
Paper from
responsible sources
FSC® C015829

V&A Publishing

Supporting the world's leading
museum of art and design,
the Victoria and Albert
Museum, London

Contents

Sponsor's Foreword

The Victoria and Albert Museum's internationally renowned fashion collections are a constant source of inspiration for designers, fashion houses and fashion devotees alike. Over the years Coutts has established strong links with the world of fashion and with contemporary creative talent, which supports our continuing commitment to celebrating British design excellence.

We are proud to be sponsors of *Ballgowns: British Glamour since 1950*, for which the V&A's beautiful Fashion Gallery provides a fitting context.

Foreword

It gives me great pleasure to contribute to *Ballgowns: British Glamour since 1950*. For many designers, the ballgown continues to be the highpoint of their seasonal collection, and the creativity and workmanship required to make the perfect dress for the perfect evening mean that a ballgown equally remains a special part of a woman's wardrobe.

The Victoria and Albert Museum possesses one of the world's finest fashion collections. The dresses shown in this book, and displayed in the exhibition it accompanies, represent a tour de force of the last sixty years of British style. I was fortunate enough to wear a gown by Mary Donan that is included in this collection; it is a source of great pleasure to see it displayed in such company.

Alexandra

H.R.H. Princess Alexandra, the Hon. Lady Ogilvy
President, The Friends of the Victoria and Albert Museum

Introduction: Pictures Worth a Thousand Words
Magdalene Keaney

I would describe David Hughes as a photographer in search of ideas as much as a photographer in search of pictures. By this I mean it's often something abstract and outside of what we see in a given image which most interests him and which he is actually concerned with expressing or representing (fig.1). And this is curious because as a photographer who works at once, and at ease, between editorial fashion, still life and realist documentary, one might assume that the subject of Hughes' photographs are the things we see framed by his lens, as they are. His engagement with the physicality of the objects he photographs results in clever compositions, subtle meditations, structural explorations and sometimes even jokes, but it is the unexpected opportunities to tangibly respond to something more than is visual that often captivates me in his work.

That Hughes was commissioned to make these photographs by the V&A provides an interesting first point of discussion around this project. Normally images for a catalogue like this would be made by the expert and highly experienced art photography section of the museum. The aim would be precise and objective recording – information-giving without excessive distraction. Commissioning Hughes challenges and extends this conventional approach. While the book still functions as a visual record with a scholarly intent, the nature of the brief becomes creative and interpretive. Readers may enjoy Hughes' photographs in their own right as well as the connoisseurship relating to the history of dress. Future generations may come to value the publication as a photo book as much as an exhibition catalogue or collection highlights guide.

The precedent for the V&A's foresight in commissioning may have been Irving Penn's photo essay *Inventive Paris Clothes*, published in 1977 as a collaboration with Metropolitan Museum curator and *Vogue* editor Diana Vreeland (fig.3). Penn was inspired by Vreeland's costume exhibition *The 10s, 20s, 30s*, drawn from the Metropolitan Museum collection. In Penn's case it was not a commission but a personal desire to 'study those clothes on the ground glass of a camera' that led to the 'practical matter' of making a book.[1]

Penn noted that 'the Museum's staff generously improvised a studio for me in one of their unused galleries'.[2] For conservation and security reasons Hughes photographed garments in a makeshift studio at the V&A's storage facility at Blythe House in west London. That Hughes utilizes a plain backdrop and mannequins, as did Penn, is as much a practicality as anything – museum collection items are not permitted to be worn by living models. Yet in both bodies of work the mannequin is posed and photographed in expressive and dramatic ways, so that rather than receding into the background it becomes important to the way the pictures relate to each other as a sequence or series.

Drawing attention to his use of the busts Penn makes something of a joke, noting in his brief foreword to the book that the clothes 'had been conveniently hung on uncomplaining plastic dummies'. I've often considered that he continued the pun into the pages of *Inventive Paris Clothes*. My eye wonders if it is imagining a particular hand, arm or leg as more human than plastic in texture and shape on this mannequin? If the stocking-covered heads, a Vreeland

1 *Previous page:*
   From 'Face for Radio?',
   Ponystep *magazine,*
   Issue 1 Spring/Summer 2011
   David Hughes

2 *Erdem's 'Rumina' silk*
   evening dress with appliqué,
   quilting and beading,
   Autumn/Winter 2008-9
   David Hughes

trademark, would allow for the sinuous feminine neckline and soft lips I can't help but see on that one? Penn was a master in the darkroom and it would have been easy for him to splice together negatives of the real and the unreal to create such playful effects. The ambiguity is appealing in any case.

Hughes too seems interested in a Galatea effect,[3] so that in the photograph of the magnificent Giles gown (pl.21), for example, white arms stretch out of the black shimmering pleated layers as though reaching for life through their fingertips. And in that of the Erdem dress (fig.2, pl.23), with the lighting across the torso and fine details such as the hand holding the underside of a book, the composure and pose suggest a demure character from a Jane Austen novel, half coming to life.

For both photographers the transformation is never complete and the glamour is a tension between animate and inanimate. In Penn's images, plastic surfaces catch and reflect the light, metal stands hold up torso forms in rigid poses. The edge of the backdrop, or a coiled cord in the corner of an image, remind us that we are in a photographic studio. Hughes breaks the spell by leaving visible the breaks between screwed-on hands and forearms, arms and shoulders, which could have been re-touched out. The limbs are prosthetics; he constructs these poses.

Another more recent project worth describing in the context of Hughes' commission is Sølve Sundsbø's photography for the 2011 Metropolitan Museum exhibition *Alexander McQueen: Savage Beauty* (figs 4,5). Again the mannequin is a key conceptual motif of the publication,

in which Sundsbø documents a large proportion of a single designer's output for an exhibition catalogue. As the archive came from the design house rather than the Metropolitan Museum collection, Sundsbø was able to work with garments on living models, yet in an inspired twist he reverses the process of coming to life. Exploiting the potential of digital photographic techniques the models he photographed wearing collection pieces in his studio become frozen alabaster on the page. Mostly headless, all featureless, traces of skin colour tones at the elbows and fingertips, or revealed under scratches across the neckline, chest and back, are the last vestiges of flesh that remain. While some torsos also resist the reversal with a naturalness and grace of pose that could not be cast or moulded – two hands pulling a plaid jacket over exposed breasts – it is an 'exaggerated mannequinism' that Sundsbø employs.[4]

Of course in Hughes' images naturalism is disrupted by the inclusion of surrealist headpieces, the idea of set designer Vincent Olivieri who made each 'hat' individually from second-hand books in response to the particular garment it might be photographed with. These were constructed on the day of the shoot and add a contemporary layer of creative interpretation and life to both mannequin and gown. As *Ballgowns: British Glamour since 1950* is a survey that traverses six decades, this embellishment creates a unifying narrative, all be it a wonderfully unpredictable one. That Hughes and Olivieri used books creates a reference to a fairy-tale or story-book context befitting the grandness of the idea of the ballgown and the sense of occasion it implies. This could be an imaginary fiction as much

3 *Diana Vreeland, photographed
   by Harry Benson in front of
   'The World of Balenciaga', the
   exhibition she curated and
   installed at the Metropolitan
   Museum of Art, New York, 1973
   Harry Benson*

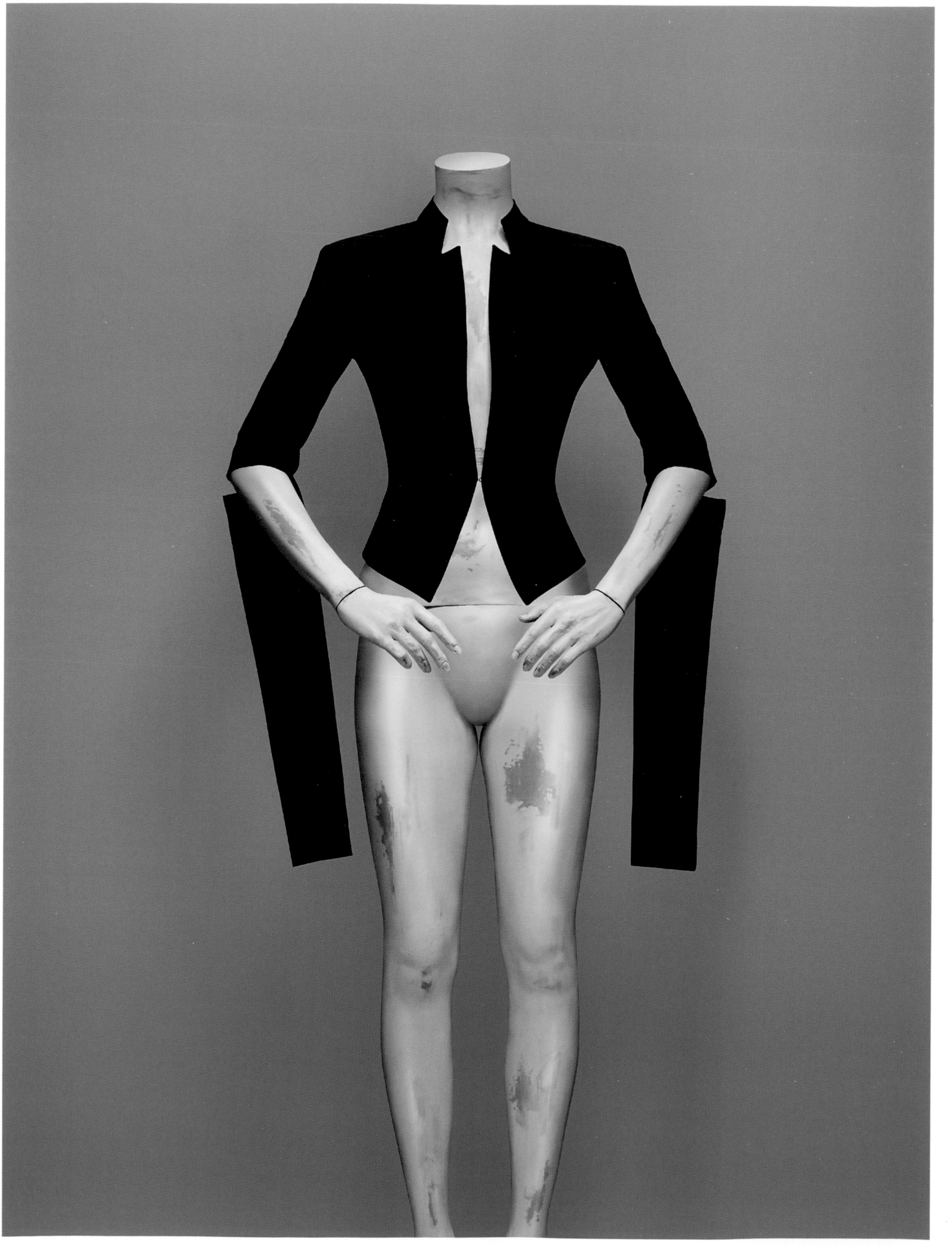

as the real story or biography of the previous owner of the gown. The use of second-hand books also represents the new function of the dresses as historical artefacts now collected and stored by the V&A, itself a seat of learning and a repository of books and knowledge.

I once read rock musician Patti Smith's description of her love of ballgowns for 'their cut, their architecture'. The sentiment came to mind when I saw Hughes' photographs, which also display a sophisticated appreciation of the design and fabrication of the ballgown. It returns me to the idea of the importance to Hughes of that which is unseen; these images provoke consideration of the craftsmanship, the precise technical decisions and relationships involved in their making, which are necessarily hidden in exquisite dresses made to look effortlessly beautiful. Hughes' use of Olivieri's headpieces contributes to this awareness. Painted, folded, cut, rolled so carefully, they mimic the laborious and unique structure of the ballgowns themselves and suggest that not only mannequins, but also the design process itself, might possess a life of its own, an energy. Looking at them I imagine letters falling off the page, flying through the air, seeking new combinations, rhythms and forms. If spoken, they would make the sounds of hundreds of hours of construction, stitching, cutting, threading, sewing, the sounds of human breath, touch and concentration.

The Magic Circle: Designing the Ballgown
Oriole Cullen

In 1953 London newspapers reported that 'Britain's first couturier'[1] Norman Hartnell (1901–1979) had been ordered by his doctors to take several days' rest, as he was suffering from exhaustion due to the overwhelming number of orders for dresses for the forthcoming coronation. This parade of monarchy and pageantry, which heralded the future reign of Queen Elizabeth II, was a welcome celebration for many after the years of austerity that followed the Second World War, and this most spectacular of ceremonies signalled a hoped-for return to a period of prosperity.

Hartnell was not only responsible for the Queen's own coronation robe but also those worn by all the female members of the royal party, as well as the re-design of the robes to be worn by the Peeresses of the Realm and their caps of state. As Hartnell's biographer Michael Pick recorded,

6   *Norman Hartnell's design for the Queen's coronation dress, 1953*

7   *Norman Hartnell in his salon at 26 Bruton Street, Mayfair, London, 1963*

'The workrooms ran at full capacity and the company had to rent extra space outside its main building. Security surrounding the design of the Coronation dress and the dresses for the royal family was strict and difficult to maintain'.[2]

Hartnell's atelier employed 350 people and had its own large in-house embroidery studio, where all the highly specialized designs were executed. A cream duchesse satin Hartnell dress with pink beading, worn by glamorous actress Lilli Palmer to one of the coronation balls, shows Hartnell's signature embroidery techniques (pl.2). But it was the coronation dress, with its all-over lavish embroidery, which epitomized for many the fairy-tale aspect of the young Queen in her crown and ballgown (fig.6).

The eyes of the world were focused on the coronation, which in turn drew attention to London's reputation for designing grand dresses for formal occasions. High society still revolved around the royal calendar. As such, there was good and regular business for many of the couture houses that had established themselves around London's exclusive Mayfair district (fig.7). While Parisian evening gowns were seen as the epitome of elegance, London was known for dresses that encapsulated nostalgia and romance. Indeed, when the Incorporated Society of London Fashion Designers took its trade show to the United States in 1960, journalist Ernestine Carter commented, 'The show had been christened Tweeds and Tiaras in deference to the American illusion that English women spent their days on the moors and their evenings at Buckingham Palace'.[3] At the turn of the decade, with regard to the clientele of British couturiers, this was not so far from the truth.

8   *Left: Debutantes at Queen
    Charlotte's Birthday Ball at
    Grosvenor House Hotel,
    London, May 1952*

9   *Right: Models pose wearing
    the creations of the Society
    of London Fashion Designers
    at a fashion show in London,
    September 1955*

10 *Below: Debutantes learning
    how to curtsey for their
    presentation at court, 1952*

The majority of formal balls in London took place during 'the season', which operated during the summer months. The London season was established in the seventeenth century, at the time of the Restoration, as a way of introducing young women from aristocratic backgrounds – later known as debutantes or 'debs' – into society in order to meet suitable husbands. By the mid-twentieth century the season hinged around such traditional events as the Royal Academy Summer Exhibition, Queen Charlotte's Birthday Ball, the Epsom Derby and other sporting occasions such as Ascot and the Henley and Cowes regattas. Until 1958 the season included the presentation of debutantes at court. Each debutante was required to be attired in a white evening gown with a train and elbow-length white gloves, to enter the throne room and to curtsey on presentation to the monarch (fig.10). Former debutante Fiona MacCarthy recalled:

We were trained to make the curtsey, which was by no means a perfunctory bob, more a low, sweeping gesture. The left knee needed to be locked behind the right, allowing a graceful descent with head erect, hands by your side. We learned the technique from Madame Vacani, a dancing teacher who held a kind of royal warrant for the curtsey. [4]

Janey Ironside (d.1983), fashion designer and later head of the fashion department at the Royal College of Art, described the early 1950s in her atelier and the production of the archetypal ballgown:

Eighty per cent of the ball dresses were ordered with tight, strapless bodices and immensely full long skirts. The top layer was usually of organza or some light fabric, and the three (at least) layers of net underneath were gathered until the waistband could accommodate no more ... Storing them was a problem. Just before Queen Charlotte's Ball we could not turn round for these enormous white puff-balls. [5]

Alongside Hartnell a number of established London couturiers including Peter Russell, Jo Mattli, Hardy Amies, John Cavanagh and Victor Stiebel were favoured by the debutantes (and their mothers), who would attend a continuous round of parties and balls, night after night. Each year British *Vogue* would highlight the Debs of the Season. In 1952 it noted Miss Rosamund Christie's 'coming out ball' (so-called as it referred to 'coming out' onto the social scene), held at Glyndebourne, then a private opera house. She wore a pale

11 *John Cavanagh with a sketchbook of ballgown designs, London 1950s*

12 *Hardy Amies photographs two of his models, wearing his creations, March 1960*

blue organza dress, 'the skirt a whirl of pleating', [6] by Hardy Amies (1909–2003). Amies was to take over the mantel of Hartnell when he retired, subsequently becoming official dressmaker to the Queen in 1955.

Queen Charlotte's Birthday Ball, established in 1928 to raise funds for Queen Charlotte's Hospital in London, involved an elaborate pageant. The debutantes would all advance to curtsey to the hostess of the Ball, who subsequently cut a giant birthday cake (fig. 8). The ball continued to be held until 1976, with intermittent revivals in the following decades, but by the 1950s it was already viewed as outdated by some of the young attendees. In 1952 firecrackers were found to be concealed inside the cake, timed to go off as it was cut. As a result, in 1955 the cake was accompanied by its own security detail. As the Ball's president, Margarita, Lady Howard de Walden, stated, 'Just to be safe I decided a detective was a wise precaution ... you never know what these young men will get up to next'.[7]

The generation that had come of age following the war included designers such as Mary Quant (b.1934), who opened her King's Road shop Bazaar in 1955, and Marion Foale (b.1939) and Sally Tuffin (b.1938), who established their eponymous label in 1961. These designers were known for their off-the-peg boutique fashions, which were a world away from couture. Debutantes no longer wished to dress as carbon copies of their mothers and, by day at least, they could now choose to wear the mini-dresses produced by these of-the-moment designers. For formal evening events, however, they still frequented the couture fashion houses or private dressmakers.

Younger than Hartnell and his peers, John Cavanagh (1914–2003) had trained in Paris under Molyneux and worked at Balmain before returning to London to establish his own couture house in Curzon Street in 1952 (fig.11). Having worked in Paris, Cavanagh was well aware of the demands of the couture client but often received unusual requests of a particularly British nature. One titled client chose a dress from his collection and requested that her own fabric be cut up and used: some eighteenth-century golden-yellow Chinese embroidered wall-hangings duly arrived at the atelier. Another client would choose several designs and then have fabric samples sent to her home to ensure she didn't clash with her furnishings.[8] For all London couturiers, designing around heirloom jewellery was another key factor and Lindsay Evans Robertson, personal assistant to John Cavanagh from 1961 to 1965, recalled trying to match a particular shade of satin to 'a set of aquamarines the size of gobstoppers'.[9]

Aware of the social changes that were occurring during the late 1950s and early 1960s, Cavanagh decided to produce a boutique line to attract younger customers.[10] This was also a financially astute move, for while couture still had a loyal customer base in existing clients it was becoming harder to attract new clientele. Cavanagh employed Alfredo Bouret, who had been a fellow designer at Balmain, to set up a boutique department alongside the couture. Bouret had a wonderful sense of colour, used beautiful fabrics and designed very simple, clean-lined evening wear that could be fitted in a single session, as opposed to the numerous fittings and appointments required with

13 *The Duchess of Cornwall
as a debutante in a
Bellville Sassoon dress, 1965*

couture pieces.[11] These Cavanagh boutique designs, such as the black petal dress, with its impeccable tailoring and carefully cut out flowers to conceal the zip (pl.5), adhered to London Model House standards,[12] which ensured a high quality finish close to that of couture, including hand-sewn hems and hand-finished zips. The boutique lines designed by couturiers were far removed from the boutique culture of Carnaby Street and the King's Road.

In 1953 former debutante Belinda Bellville established her own design house, Bellville et Cie. Five years later Royal College of Art graduate David Sassoon (b.1932) joined the company, which was later renamed Bellville Sassoon. Sassoon recalled, 'This concentrated calendar of dedicated partying demanded a sophisticated and glamorous wardrobe, and Belinda, who'd been a deb herself, spotted a gap in the market for young, pretty debutante dresses that were also exclusive'.[13] Bellville pieces had a wide appeal. In 1963 the Queen held a ball for 2000 people at Windsor Castle to celebrate the wedding of her cousin, Princess Alexandra, to the Hon. Angus Ogilvy. Amongst the guests the *Daily Telegraph* noted in particular Lady Pamela Hicks, who wore a Bellville dress of white Grecian chiffon beneath a green evening coat. Lady Aberdare also wore a Bellville creation, in an orange and pink floral pattern that reflected the trend for bright colours and bold prints. Other guests included the Duchess of Rutland, in a glitter-embroidered lace gown by Hartnell, and Anne, Countess of Rosse, in an emerald satin and white tulle ballgown by Victor Stiebel.[14]

Sassoon, like Hartnell and Cavanagh, would be asked to create dresses that showed off jewellery to its best effect,

a design process that he was especially in tune with. Many of his British clients had significant collections that had been passed down from one generation to another. Formal evening occasions provided an increasingly rare opportunity for these magnificent pieces to be worn. In order to minimize theft or loss, many owners devised ingenious ways to avoid transporting pieces to the couturier. Sassoon recalled how one woman put on her chosen necklace at home and then drew around the edge with a pen, leaving the outline on her skin, so that he would have a sense of the necklace when she visited the atelier. There were also occasions on which he was required to go to the repository where a client's jewellery collection was stored. One titled lady sent him to Garrards (the London jewellery house established in 1735) to select a pair of diamond earrings to match her dress. Thinking it would be a case of choosing between two pairs, he was amazed when the jewellers brought out a large leather case containing 22 astounding pairs of diamond earrings.[15]

By the late 1970s the private ball, held in country houses or grand London residences, began to be replaced by the charity ball. Accessible through the purchase of a ticket, these events had a more eclectic and international guest list, which saw musicians, actors, writers and celebrities mixing with members of the aristocracy. Often these parties would lead on to a late night at Annabel's, London's famed nightclub named by proprietor Mark Birley after his then-wife Annabel, granddaughter of one of London's most formidable hostesses of the early twentieth century, Edith, Lady Londonderry.

14 *Zandra Rhodes' evening*
ensemble of black quilted
satin bodice, pleated
gold lamé skirt and panniers
over black tulle, 1981
David Hughes

Youth culture and the traditional London social scene, which had existed on parallel planes, had begun to merge by the 1970s. In sartorial terms the new, relaxed and natural approach to fashion saw clients demanding a less stiff and formal way of dressing for evening occasions. While newspapers and magazines such as *Tatler* and *Vogue* still reported on high society events, the magazine editorials reflected what was happening in the world of high fashion, with loose free-flowing silhouettes now favoured for eveningwear. In order to remain relevant an increasing number of couturiers began to follow Cavanagh's example, designing boutique lines that could now be bought off the peg. In 1971 even the young Princess Anne purchased a mustard-yellow evening gown with embroidered lattice bodice from the boutique range at Bellville Sassoon (pl.8). As Ernestine Carter observed in 1974, 'Couture can no longer survive on its own ... Hardy Amies and Norman Hartnell have understood this and both have entered the field of ready-to-wear'.[16]

A new generation of London designers, such as Zandra Rhodes, Bill Gibb, Ossie Clark and Yuki, joined the likes of Bellville Sassoon in offering more wearable, less structured gowns that could be worn for formal occasions. Like Bellville Sassoon, these designers, while realising that the future of their business lay in off-the-peg garments, continued to produce couture or special order pieces. They all understood the importance of the statement dress. As *Harpers & Queen* reported in 1974, 'In the evening Bill Gibb's clothes are frothy extravaganzas. Bold splashes of colour, layer upon layer of luxurious materials, perfect detailing,

make you feel sophisticated and slightly spoiled'.[17] Zandra Rhodes was known for her work as a textile designer in the 1960s but by the late 1970s it was her unique garments that were in great demand for formal occasions. Fellow designer Jean Muir's view was that 'Zandra, at the end of the day, makes the most beautiful evening dresses in the world' (fig.14, pl.14).[18]

The early 1980s saw a renewed focus on the royal family with the emergence of Diana, Princess of Wales, the young, attractive wife of the heir to the throne. British *Vogue* reported, 'Everyone wishes to dance these days and it's not simply disco dressing. There has been the glitter and quiver of tiaras and a great new demand for truly flattering dressed-up-to-the-nines dresses'.[19] Inspired by the celebratory mood created by the new Princess, Zandra Rhodes designed her Modern Renaissance collection in 1981. She wanted to take the opulence and drama of an earlier age and translate this into spectacular formal garments that were both light and easy to wear. As such, her gold lamé and black satin pieces were available in a range of separate, interchangeable bodices and super-light skirts supported by panniers, which did away with the need for layered underskirts (pl.14).

Despite social change, the market for couture continued. The 1980s saw a closer relationship between the work of couture designers and contemporary fashion, united by strong colours and dramatic silhouettes. In 1978 two new designers had established their design labels: Bruce Oldfield (b.1950) and Victor Edelstein (b.1945). Oldfield, young and attractive, who had worked his way up from

15 *Bruce Oldfield's gold lamé evening gown, worn by Diana, Princess of Wales at the London premiere of the James Bond film* A View To A Kill *at the Empire, Leicester Square, London, July 1985*

16 *The Duke and Duchess of Cambridge at the BAFTA Brits to Watch event at the Belasco Theatre in Los Angeles, California, July 2011*

an underprivileged background, created sophisticated and glamorous evening wear that epitomized the forthcoming decade (fig.15). Of his clientele, which comprised a heady mix of stars and aristocrats, Oldfield later said in 1987, 'I knew exactly who my clients were and I knew they wanted what I was making. I owe a great debt to some of them who have been continuously supportive – Charlotte Rampling, Joan Collins, Stefanie Powers, Bianca Jagger, Angelica Houston, Lulu, Joanna Lumley, Viscountess Astor, the Duchess of Kent, and latterly the Princess of Wales. Between them they have steered the Bruce Oldfield name into prominence'.[20]

Victor Edelstein, formerly designer at Christian Dior in London, also dressed an impressive list of clients including Princess Michael of Kent and Anne, Lady Heseltine. He too designed eveningwear for Princess Diana, including the celebrated midnight-blue velvet dress that she wore to the White House in Washington in 1985, the night she danced with John Travolta.

By the mid-1990s, as the fashion world realised the potential for product placement with so-called 'red carpet' appearances, a new focus for formal dressing presented itself, particularly glamorous events associated with the entertainment industry, such as 'the Oscars', the Academy Awards ceremony in Hollywood. British designers Vivienne Westwood (b.1941) and John Galliano (b.1960) were electrifying the world of high fashion with their unique, extravagant couture shows in Paris, often featuring elaborate ballgowns (fig.18). Other designers championed a new streamlined approach to fashion, which saw the column dress become a popular choice for eveningwear. For Princess Diana, who appeared on many red carpet events associated with the charities she supported, Catherine Walker (1945–2010) was a favourite choice. Born in France and self-taught as a designer in London, Walker became well known for her clean silhouettes and perfectly tailored garments. She was credited with creating a sophisticated, assured look for the newly independent Princess, following her divorce from Prince Charles in 1996.

A noticeable difference in style had by now emerged between cutting-edge British fashion and the more traditional couture houses. Yet underpinning the work of even that most avant-garde of designers, Alexander McQueen (1969–2010), who established his own line in 1993, were undeniably British traditions: impeccable tailoring and an acknowledgment of the importance of a dramatic gown as a fashion statement. McQueen's conceptual dresses were often worn on the red carpet by women who had a strong sense of personal style and were unafraid to break with traditional notions of evening dress. Fashion editor Isabella Blow was known for her wardrobe of spectacular McQueen designs, as is the Hon. Daphne Guinness, who continues to wear McQueen (fig.17). In 2002 the label was still seen as a very daring choice when actress Gwyneth Paltrow shocked audiences at that year's Oscars by wearing a full-skirted McQueen dress with a sheer black bodice. Today, with designer Sarah Burton at the helm, the house of Alexander McQueen has gone on to design for events at the heart of the British establishment, including both evening dresses

(fig.16) and the magnificent wedding dress for Catherine, Duchess of Cambridge on the occasion of her marriage to Prince William in 2011.

The statement evening dress is no longer a garment that is worn to a private event and possibly photographed in an official portrait. Dresses worn on today's red carpet are photographed from every angle by the world's press. No designer is more aware of this than Roland Mouret. Mouret (b.1961), like Catherine Walker, was born in France, but established his design house in London in 1998. He came to international prominence in the early 2000s when his work was worn by a number of international stars at red carpet events. In his opinion, 'The ballgown ... has a reality in this country. It is something that exists, through events, there is a customer, it is something that works ... it's quite amazing to see how really creative a designer can be'.[21]

The contemporary client now looks for a dress that reflects her own persona, or how she would like to be perceived, as opposed to an extravagant other-worldly creation. Many designers agree that a client will come to them for a special commission because they are familiar with their work, identify a mutual sense of style, and want something that carries the recognizable stamp of a particular designer – such as Giles Deacon (b.1969). Credited with injecting high-octane glamour into British fashion, Deacon founded his own label, GILES, in 2003 and often designs 'structured big-entrance' dresses, aimed at women who want to be noticed.[22] As Deacon noted of his 'Carwash Dress' from his Spring/Summer 2007 collection (pl.21), 'The carwash is a perfect example of an archetypal GILES dress, not just an occasion dress – it has a sharp, graphic silhouette that is incredibly lightweight and the movement of the skirt has enormous drama, which is a million miles away from a soft wispy evening gown'.[23] The dress itself was inspired by the very modern experience of 'sitting in the car whilst it was being washed in the carwash on City Road',[24] yet the movement in the dress also looks back to the nineteenth-century ballroom scene in Luchino Visconti's beautifully nostalgic film *The Leopard* of 1963.[25]

Over the past 60 years the ballgown has retained a special place within the world of fashion. In Britain, the presence of royalty has preserved grand evening occasions that often retain an air of formality with regard to etiquette. And while younger members of the royal family are gradually introducing a more relaxed approach to traditional events, the current generation of designers, trained and based in London, are as aware of the impact that an incredible evening gown can have, as the designers of previous decades. One such designer is Gareth Pugh (b.1981), known for his immaculately constructed, theatrical garments made up in fabrics such as mink and parachute silk, plastic and PVC. Pugh, the latest designer in a long tradition of fashion-as-performance-art that looks back to McQueen, Galliano and Westwood, succinctly sums up the Cinderella effect that the ballgown represents: 'That's what fashion's about ... you're transforming yourself from something that you are to maybe something that you want to be ... that's the crux of what we do, it's selling people a dream'.[26]

Ballgowns: The Rituals of Dressing Up
Sonnet Stanfill

Since the 1950s, occasions for wearing formal attire have evolved from the private event to the public parade. In the post-war period, as Europe struggled toward recovery, extravagant, exclusive balls provided a glittering backdrop for splendid couture gowns, so helping to stimulate sartorial consumption and aspiration in Britain. Coming out balls, where young women were formally introduced to society, were often the first occasion on which to wear a grand gown. Participation in 'the season' was long considered a significant rite of passage for young, well-born British women.[1] In the last decades of the twentieth century, this tradition became less important as other entertainments became established. The charity ball, for example, open to all, became popular and the subject of increasing press interest.

Today it is the red carpet that acts as the most important site of fashionable splendour. As fashion designer David Sassoon observed, from the 1990s couturiers 'scrambled to dress stars for red carpet events, which now received global press coverage on television, in newspapers and in magazines ... It was the cult of celebrity married to the new opiate of the people – shopping – with rampant consumerism at all levels of the market'.[2] An example of so-called 'red carpet dressing' is actress Annette Bening's choice of Stella McCartney to wear to the New York Film Critics Circle Awards in January 2011 (fig.21, pl.30). As the red carpet's paparazzi-lined path leaves little room for misjudgement, today's celebrities dress with particular care. According to the designer Roland Mouret, 'For the red carpet, an actress needs to wear what is right ... but at the same time [has] to keep her identity',[3] a duality illustrated by the Mouret design worn by actress Maggie Gyllenhaal for the Golden Globe Awards in Los Angeles, January 2010 (fig.20).

Carefully chosen for special occasions, a ballgown should not only flatter the wearer and demonstrate her sense of style but also illustrate an understanding of the significance of the event to which it is worn. This essay focuses on five gowns worn for a range of evening occasions by women of different ages. The designer/client relationships they represent all appear to have possessed a warm, respectful camaraderie. These associations reflect the importance of a designer's tact and discretion, particularly for clients in the public eye. Equally, the loyalty of a fashionable client can be crucial to sustaining a designer's career. For as Hardy Amies stated, the 'best discipline for a designer is a customer with taste'.[4] The following histories of fittings, the purchasing and wearing of ballgowns for important occasions are tangible evidence of the British reverence for dressing up.

A momentous occasion for 23-year-old Jill Slotover, now Lady Ritblat, was the ball hosted in 1966 to celebrate her engagement. Ritblat, then a recently qualified barrister and now arts patron, from the 1960s collected a wardrobe of ready-to-wear and couture outfits by leading designers such as Christian Dior, Biba, Yves Saint Laurent and Giorgio Armani. She had ordered an evening dress of pink Swiss organza from Belinda Bellville and David Sassoon's popular Infanta collec-

19 Previous page: *David Sassoon's design drawing for the Bellville Sassoon pink embroidered organza evening dress entitled 'Candida', 1964*

20 *Actress Maggie Gyllenhaal in RM by Roland Mouret attending the 67th Annual Golden Globe Awards in Los Angeles, California, January 2010*

21 *Actress Annette Bening, wearing a Stella McCartney design, with her husband Warren Beatty at the 2010 New York Film Critics Circle Awards in New York, January 2011*

22 *Yuki's raspberry-pink silk chiffon kaftan dress, 1972, modelled by Gayle Hunnicutt for British* Vogue, *October 1973*

tion two years earlier.[5] The dress features the slim, columnar silhouette popular for eveningwear in the early 1960s. In explaining her appreciation of it, Ritblat said:

I wore it to one or two of the magnificent balls and galas which were frequent in the 1960s, and in 1966, when my future and dashing uncle-in-law, Selim Zilkha, gave a ball to celebrate my engagement to his nephew, Elie, I decided that I could not find anything more suitable to wear than this dress.[6]

The gown's clean, straight line dazzles with tour de force embroidery of crystal drop beads suspended within a tear-shaped pattern. Its delicate pink hue was then becoming fashionable; several of the designs from the 1964 Bellville Sassoon collection were shown in this colour. David Sassoon's original drawing includes a swatch of the silk organza used, which came from the Swiss textile firm Naef & Co. (fig.19, pl.6). Ritblat stated that her mother paid for the gown, since the £1000 price tag was more than she herself earned in a year.

Bellville Sassoon's ballgown is a couture design, meaning it was made to measure, specifically for the client. Though Paris is the birthplace of the haute couture tradition, London's own couture industry thrived from the early twentieth century.[7] The long established ritual of buying couture involves multiple visits to a designer's salon for fittings – all the more important for a very expensive garment. During these visits careful measurements of the client are taken and a toile, or pattern, of the dress is made. Subsequent visits confirm the precise details of the finished garment. These fittings take place within the designer's salon, often with an ambiance of a small private club, which both reflects a designer's taste and serves as an oasis for the clients. Ritblat recalls the atmosphere at Bellville Sassoon's premises in London's Cadogan Lane:

The salon was unusual, as most of the salons my mother took me to ... were gilded, upholstered and carpeted, and all were in prime locations in Mayfair. It was an adventure to go to a very small and unpretentious salon, a former stable in a mews in Belgravia ... I found it exciting and new.[8]

Jill Ritblat married and moved to Switzerland, where balls and galas were infrequent. Consequently, she sold many of her Bellville Sassoon gowns, noting, 'The only one I kept was this one for its sentimental value'.[9]

Like Jill Ritblat, actress Gayle Hunnicutt saved the ballgowns that for her held special significance, including an example by the Japanese-born, London-based Gnyuki Torimaru (b.1940), who designed under his label Yuki. Torimaru's unique training included textile engineering, then architecture followed by a course in pattern-cutting at the London College of Fashion. Torimaru moved to Paris in 1969 to work as a designer for Pierre Cardin, and established his own label in London in 1972. The growing trend toward informality that began in the early 1960s became more pronounced by the end of that decade, by which time even trousers were accepted as formal attire for women. The corseted waists and bell-shaped skirts of the 1950s and the trim, tailored silhouette of the early-to-mid 1960s were replaced by a flowing, draped line. The loose fit of the colourful kaftan became a fashionable eveningwear choice.

Gayle Hunnicutt wore a kaftan-shaped gown to a ball at Windsor Castle in the early 1970s, an event that she described as 'thrilling and exciting'. The dress is cut with a curved hem, which is slightly padded round the edges; a delightful, unexpected detail. Its clean line is broken only by the bow at the small of the wearer's back. What sets this dress apart are its raspberry hue and plunging back, making it ideal for a dramatic entrance (fig.22, pl.12). Hunnicutt described the appeal of a Yuki dress: 'Yuki's clothes were very grand, they were very special and unusual but they were *wearable*. You never felt, as I have done in other evening clothes, "Am I going to be able to get out of the car?" They have a fluidity which I found easy to wear'.[10]

Torimaru sold his clothes initially through Harvey Nichols and through boutiques such as Lucienne Philips. While a number of clients visited him at his workroom, he received special couture clients such as Gayle Hunnicutt and Margaret Thatcher at his home in Chester Square, which was decorated in the manner of the Regency period.[11]

Yuki's designs were wardrobe staples for Hunnicutt throughout the 1970s. She wore his gowns frequently to attend film premieres and other high profile gatherings. Recalling the panache with which Hunnicutt wore his clothing, Yuki stated:

I escorted Gayle on many occasions and she always looked like a great star, and so she was. I remember particularly when we arrived at her husband David Hemmings' film premiere in a Lamborghini in Leicester Square. Gayle wore an apple-green silk georgette evening dress which I had designed for the occasion, she wore her red hair piled up in a dramatic way and the press photographers went crazy.[12]

In addition to wearing her pink chiffon gown to Windsor Castle, Hunnicutt modelled it for the October 1973 issue of British *Vogue*. Photographed by Henry Clarke, the image highlights the theatrical impact of Yuki's designs.

Hunnicutt later donated to the V&A 11 Yuki ensembles in a range of architectural shapes and strong colours. She was unequivocal about Yuki's influence on her wardrobe:

Yuki believed in me, both as a person and as an actress, and wanted me to look my best. I know there is always a symbiotic relationship between a woman and her designer, but I always felt that *he* was taking care of *me*. He always made sure he'd find me something wonderful to wear.[13]

Like actress Gayle Hunnicutt, Lady Heseltine created a wardrobe to accommodate a life lead in the public eye. As a museum trustee and the wife of a leading politician, she has chosen clothes appropriate for both roles and frequented the London couturier Victor Edelstein for over two decades for his classic, well crafted designs.[14] Like most long-term couture clients, she shared her couturier's views on good design, explaining, 'My taste was Victor's taste; you wouldn't go to him if it weren't'.[15]

Victor Edelstein (b.1945) was born in London to Russian parents who worked in the fashion industry. Edelstein worked for Biba in 1966, designed for Salvador in 1972 and for Christian Dior in 1975. He opened his own fashion business in 1978 focusing mainly on couture eveningwear and

wedding dresses made in luxurious fabrics with elegant surface embellishment. At his London salon, Edelstein received a mix of royalty and fashion-world sophisticates, including Diana, Princess of Wales, Princess Michael of Kent and Anna Wintour, who was to become editor-in-chief of American *Vogue*.

Lady Heseltine's initial patronage of Victor Edelstein began in the 1960s with the occasional dress bought from Lucienne Philips's influential Knightsbridge boutique, which carried Edelstein's early work. Her purchases increased in the early 1980s when, from 1983 to 1986, Lord Heseltine's position as Secretary of Defence required the couple to attend many evening events. Thus, at a time when dressing up had, for many people, become both less frequent and less grand, for the Heseltines this period was a particularly formal one. Lady Heseltine purchased this black and red silk evening dress during this period. The sleeveless and backless bodice joins a narrow waist and full-length skirt. Its columnar line, typical of eveningwear from the 1980s onwards, is accented by an oversized red and black striped bow, which seems to erupt from the small of the back (fig.23, pl.16). The bow's ties sweep down the body and trail along the floor, forcing the wearer, as Lady Heseltine recalled, to drape them over her arm when dancing.

The loyalty of clients like Lady Heseltine helped Victor Edelstein gain prominence as a couturier. His success was due in part to the atmosphere he created within his salon, one that encouraged clients to linger. Lady Heseltine recalled:

It was so easy to be his client. He always had interesting people working for him. His mews studio, not far from the V&A, was very simple: a big open room with one little changing room in the corner with a curtain. I loved going there, I always took far too long about it. One went for a half-an-hour's fitting and spent up to two hours just chatting and having coffee![16]

Lady Heseltine purchased this evening dress to wear to a friend's wedding anniversary celebration. She recalled, 'The invitation said "dress bewitchingly". Some people took this over-seriously and came dressed as witches, which was not really quite the idea'.[17] Though she referred to this dress as 'absolutely one of my all-time favourites', she admitted, 'It might have been worn just the once. It is a bit over the top ... you can't wear it to a dinner party'![18]

Like Lady Heseltine's long relationship with Victor Edelstein, Diana, Princess of Wales, patronized her couturier of choice for many years. But while Lady Heseltine was free to choose a ballgown based on her view of what suited her, dressing for a formal royal occasion requires different criteria. For an official visit to Hong Kong in 1989, the Princess commissioned a dress from French-born, London-based couturier Catherine Walker (fig.24). On such visits, royal wardrobes support an ambassadorial role, demonstrating regal splendour and the strength of British design, as well as honouring the tradition of visitors incorporating emblems of their host nation within their attire.

The Catherine Walker design studio is located in Chelsea's Sydney Street. Framed by a crisp white awning and trimmed greenery, the premises suggests an oasis of calm serenity, though royal clients such as the Princess would have been seen in their own residences. Walker, unusual as a French designer working in London, founded her business in 1976 selling children's clothing and maternity styles; the Princess's first Walker designs were maternitywear. She continued to choose Walker's elegant daywear and refined evening dresses until her death in 1997, and was buried in a Walker design.

To embellish this dress, Catherine Walker used pearls, a popular symbol of the Orient. The British firm S. Lock Ltd embroidered tens of thousands of these pearls onto the silk fabric, resulting in a soft, luminous sheen. The jaunty bolero jacket updated the dress's slim, columnar line while its high, pearl-encrusted collar earned the ensemble the moniker of the 'Elvis Dress'. Walker's simple, straight sheath is typical of the clean lines popular at the time, yet the opulence of her surface decoration and the ruff-like standing collar set this royal costume somewhat outside of fashion.

As a high profile member of the royal family, the Princess relied both on Walker's tasteful approach and her discretion. While several clients may select the same couture design, a couturier must avoid wardrobe duplications within the same social circle, a requirement all the more important for a member of the royal family. With Princess Diana as a client, Walker had numerous designs to monitor for this dress was one of many hundreds the Princess purchased from her. The designer later wrote, 'Whenever I saw the Princess in this dress, I could not help but feel that it would not be possible for anyone else ever to wear this dress and bolero. She shone in the dress and the dress shone around her in a shimmering column of glistening pearls'.[19]

Though the Princess wore the clothes of other designers in the course of her royal duties, Walker was, in the words of fashion journalist Tamsin Blanchard, 'the single most important designer in Diana's life'.[20]

While much of today's consumption of dramatic eveningwear takes place on the red carpet, there remain formal events for less public figures that still allow women to dress with extravagance. The 50th birthday party of Nicolette Kwok, founder and director of The Red Mansion Foundation promoting cultural exchange between Great Britain and China, was one such occasion. To be hosted at Tate Britain, her birthday celebration required a formal gown.

Kwok chose an evening dress by Osman Yousefzada (b. 1973), who creates carefully cut, architectural styles under his Osman label. Born to Afghani parents, Yousefzada designs for a multicultural Britain, a world away from the exclusive circles catered to by previous generations of designer. He clarifies, 'I see myself as very British ... I'm a product of multicultural England'.[21]

Although Yousefzada grew up surrounded by clothes – his mother ran a dressmaking business in Birmingham – his route into fashion was somewhat circuitous. First, he went into banking after graduating from Cambridge in 1997, and then left the City to study fashion design at London's Central Saint Martins before launching his own fashion label in 2005.

Yousefzada's smart atelier in London's New Quebec Street reflects his eclectic interests. The jewel-like space is dotted with images for inspiration, textile swatches and other visual reference. Commented one visitor, 'On the wall are prints of women in Masai clothing and tunics worn by the Kochis, a nomadic tribe from Afghanistan. Books on French couture are piled on every surface'.[22]

The designer's precise cut, carefully sourced fabrics and impeccable finish lend his work a strong craft connection, though it is a ready-to-wear label (fig.25). He does fit the occasional client, like Kwok, for special commissions. Nicolette Kwok is a long-time supporter and often attends the Osman catwalk presentations, which is where she saw the dress she chose for her birthday celebration. Kwok said, 'I never felt so totally passionate about a garment as I did about this dress when I saw it on Osman's catwalk at London Fashion Week last spring. As soon as the model set foot on the runway, I knew this was the dress I wanted to wear on my 50th'.[23]

For Kwok, the dress's strong design made it compelling and appropriate for her special event. Its bold fuchsia-pink colour is accented by a jagged 'stain' motif in royal blue across the chest. The bodice features a daring flash of skin at the waist where the fabric is cut away. The full-length skirt and textured silk and wool bouclé fabric lend the dress formality and gravitas. These features combined to create a dress with an offbeat edge that fitted well with Kwok's Oriental party theme and its art world guest list (fig.26, pl.31). She said of wearing the dress:

[It] felt great throughout the evening. As it is made of silk bouclé, it retains its shape, no matter whether you walk, sit or lie in it. The stiff material and cut made me feel quite regal, as if I was wearing a uniform, but in a good way. The dress seemed to give me shape.[24]

The dresses described here represent eveningwear choices made by women of differing ages over nearly a half-century. These varied histories suggest that women have valued the British designer's ability to craft gowns, both ready-to-wear and couture, with a high level of skill, befitting the grand occasion. The owners of these gowns relied on the discretion and judgement of their designers to create what was right for the occasion and flattering for the wearer. In some cases, lasting friendships developed. These women have embraced the designer who is able to achieve all this within the seductive atmosphere of the salon, thereby transforming a simple purchase into part of the memory of a special evening.

BALLGOWNS

1 **Unlabelled** 1950s

Previous pages: 2 **Norman Hartnell** 1953   3 **Matilda Etches** 1956

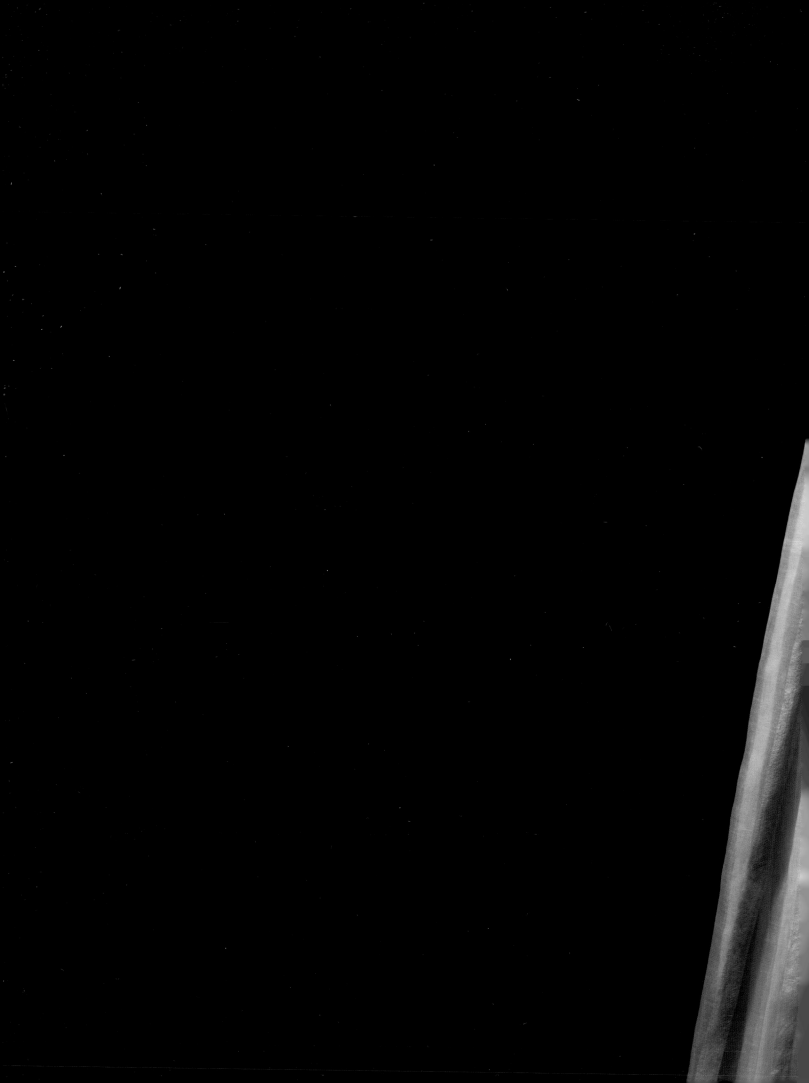

4 **Sybil Connolly** 1966   Following pages: 5 **John Cavanagh** 1965

Previous pages and opposite: 8 **Bellville Sassoon** 1968

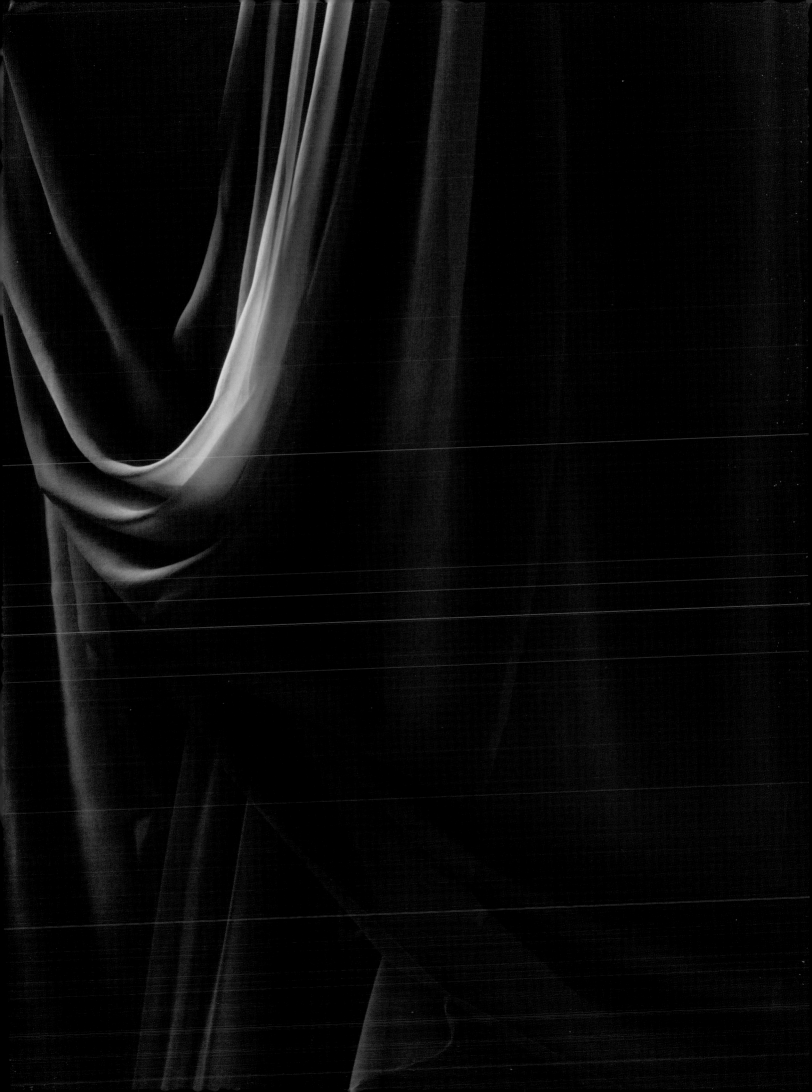

Previous pages: 9 **Mary Donan** 1969

Opposite and following pages: 10 **Cindy Beadman** late 1970s

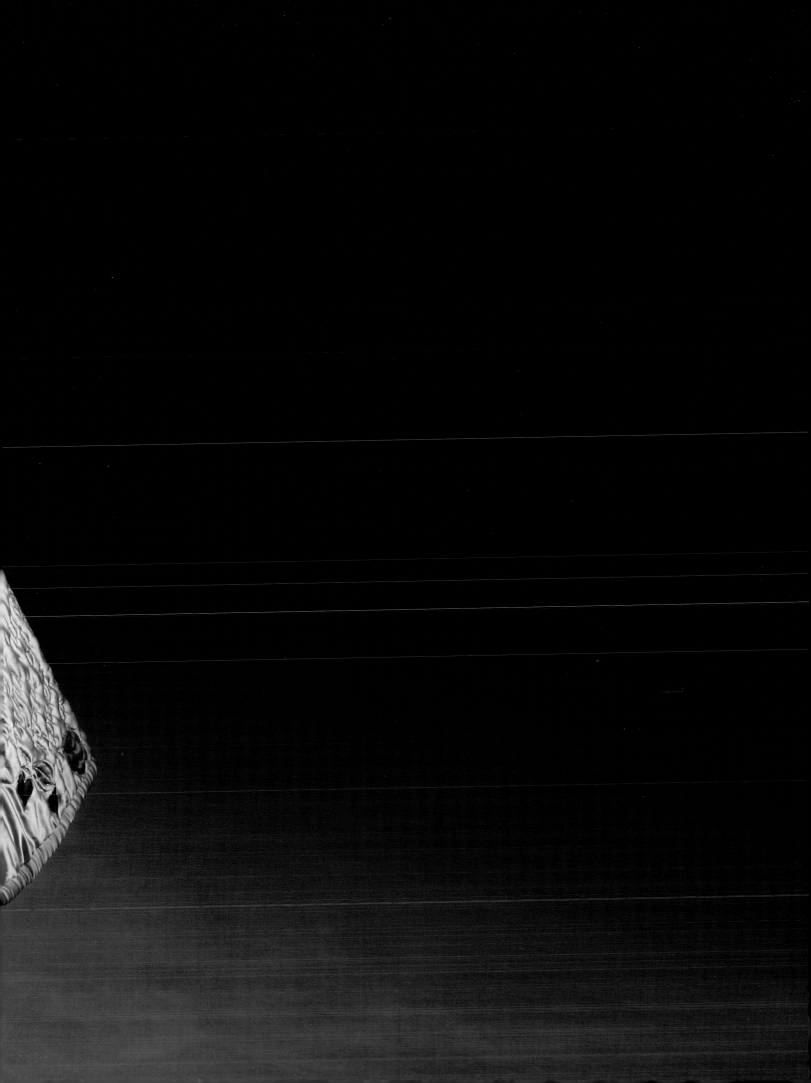

Previous pages: 11 **Hardy Amies** 1961

Opposite and following pages: 12 **Yuki** 1972

13 **Murray Arbeid** 1986

19 **Ossie Clark** 1971

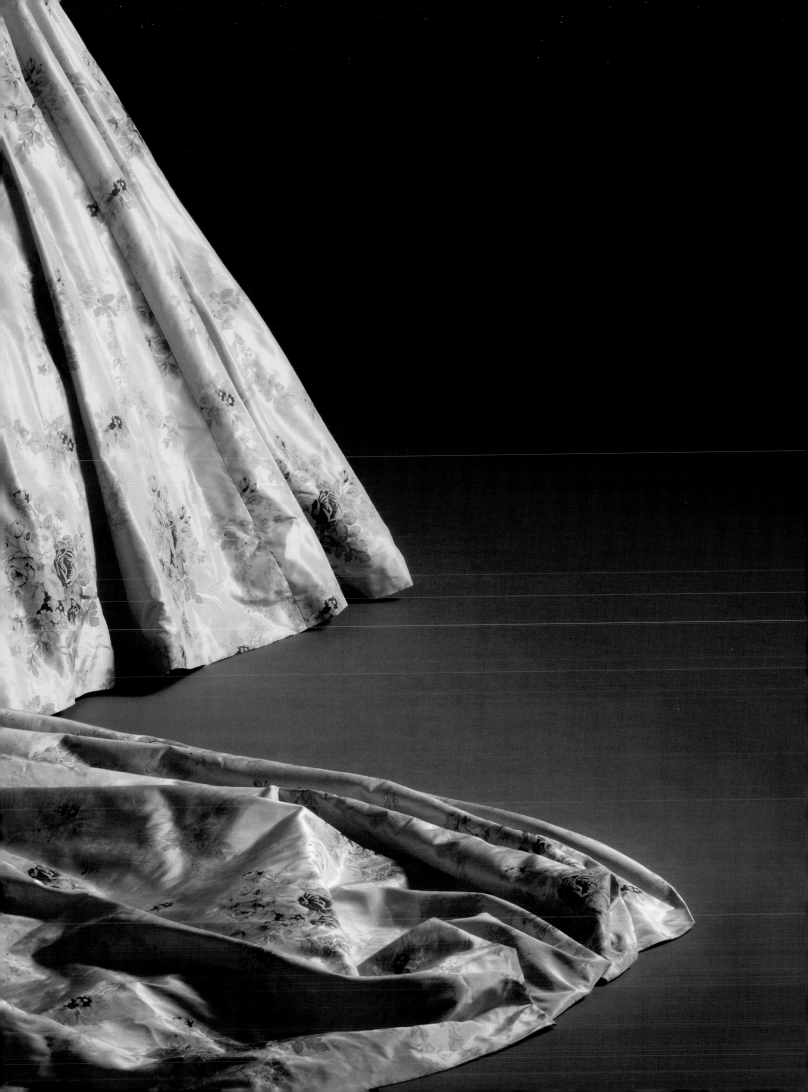

Previous pages and opposite: 20 **Elizabeth Emanuel** 1999

Previous pages and opposite: 21 **Giles Deacon** 2007

Previous pages: 22 **Roksanda Ilincic** 2009   Opposite and following pages: 23 **Erdem** 2008

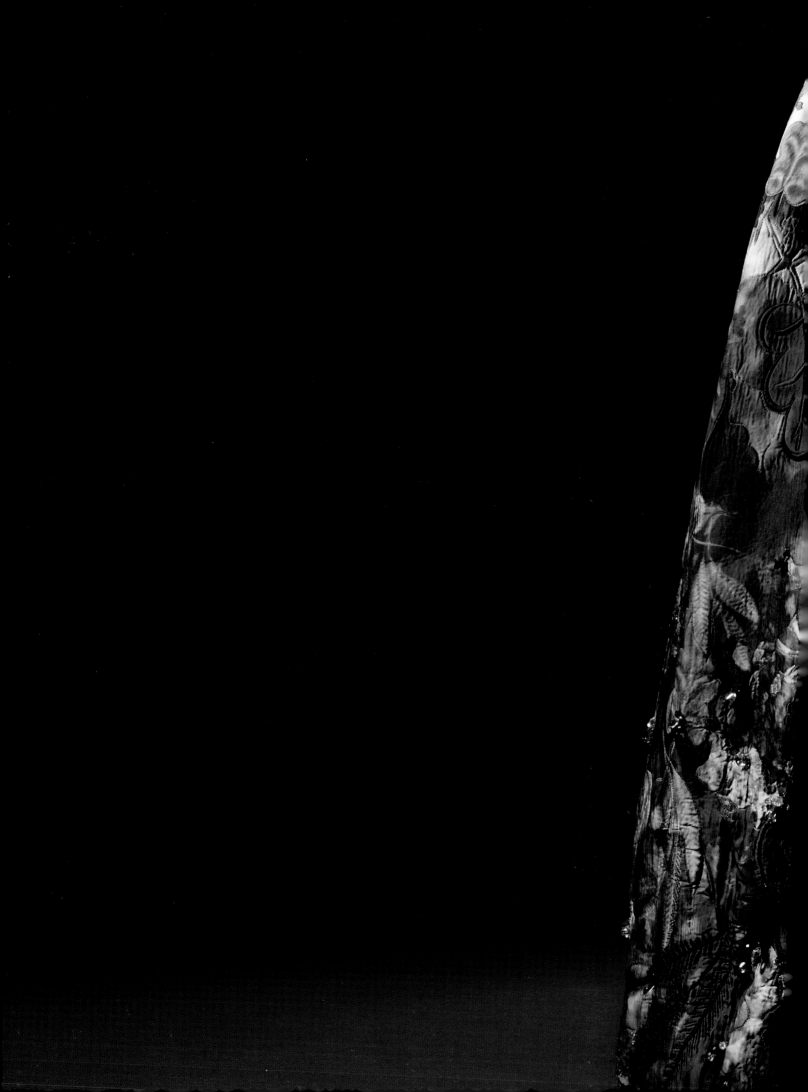

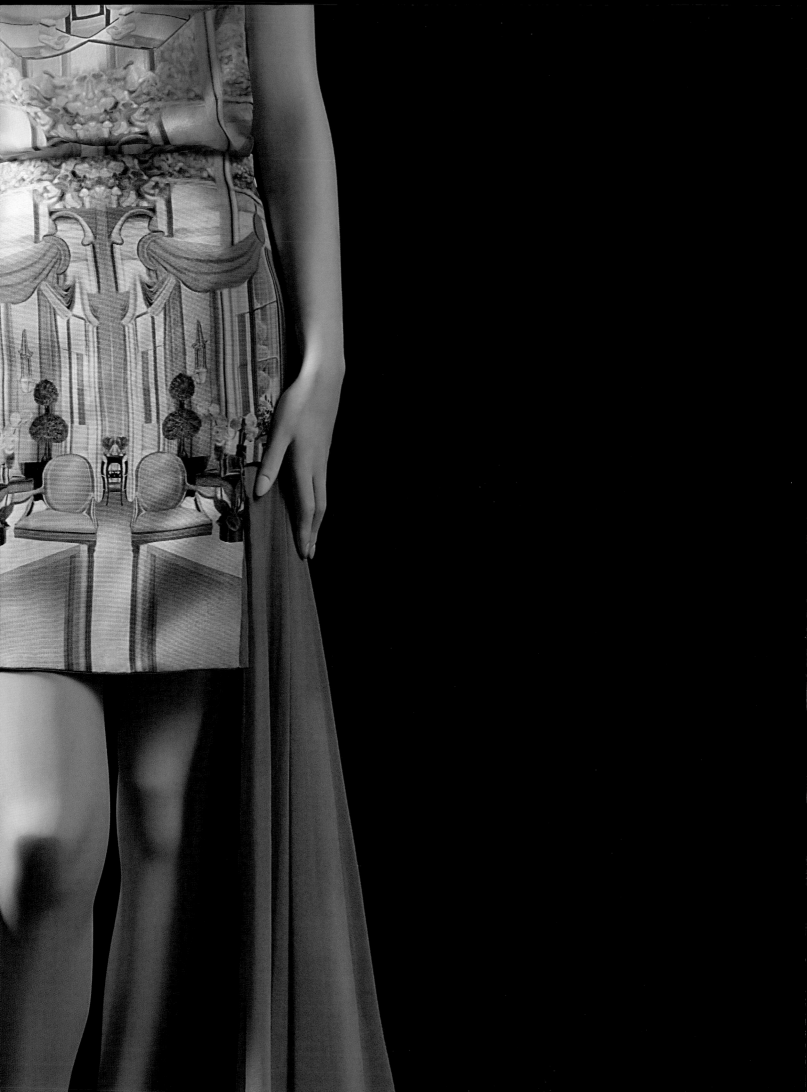

Notes

Introduction:
Pictures Worth a Thousand Words

....

1 Irving Penn and Diana Vreeland, *Inventive Paris Clothes: 1909–1939: A Photographic Essay by Irving Penn* (New York, 1977), p.7.
2 Ibid.
3 In Ovid's *Metamorphoses*, the sculptor Pygmalion falls in love with the ivory statue of the sea nymph Galatea that he has carved. He makes offerings at the altar of the goddess Venus, who grants him his wish and makes her human.
4 This is my term to describe Sundsbø's emphasis on the artificiality of the mannequin. However, I am indebted to my colleague at London College of Fashion, Judith Clark, who encouraged my thinking around Penn's use of the mannequin and whose important original research has provided a framework within which to discuss the use of mannequins in the work of Hughes, Penn and Sundsbø in this piece.

The Magic Circle:
Designing the Ballgown

....

1 Andrew Barrow, *Gossip 1920–1970* (London, 1978), p.174.
2 Michael Pick, *Bedazzled! Sixty Years of Glamour and Fashion* (London, 2007), p.162.
3 Ernestine Carter, *With Tongue in Chic* (London, 1974), p.144.
4 Fiona MacCarthy, 'Recalling the Lost Era of the Debutantes', *Daily Telegraph*, 16 March 2008.
5 Janey Ironside, *Janey* (London, 1973), p.74.
6 British *Vogue*, June 1952, pp.82–3.
7 Andrew Barrow, *Gossip 1920–1970* (London, 1978), p.184.
8 Interview with Lindsay Evans Robertson, London, 1 June 2011.
9 Ibid.
10 The first couturier to open a boutique at the front of her salon had been Elsa Schiaparelli in the immediate post-war years. She saw the potential for selling accessories in this way, which was aimed at those who could not afford couture but would disseminate the brand. Gradually other couturiers followed suit, introducing clothing alongside the smaller items.
11 Interview with Lindsay Evans Robertson, London, 1 June 2011.
12 The dresses adhered to the high standards required by the London Model House, established in 1950 by Leslie Carr-Jones and officially titled the Fashion House Group of London from 1955. It established a prestigious standing and set up the first London Fashion Weeks.
13 David Sassoon and Sinty Stemp, *The Glamour of Bellville Sassoon* (London, 2008), p.34.
14 *Daily Telegraph*, 22 April 1963.
15 Interview with David Sassoon, London, 7 April 2011.
16 Ernestine Carter, *With Tongue in Chic* (London, 1974), p.162.
17 *Harpers & Queen*, February 1974.
18 British *Vogue*, 15 March 1980, p.78.
19 Ibid.
20 Georgina Howells, *Bruce Oldfield's Season* (London, 1987), p.72.
21 Interview with Roland Mouret, London, 25 May 2011.
22 Susannah Frankel, 'Giles Deacon: the boy is back in town', *Independent*, 20 September 2010.
23 Correspondence with Giles Deacon, 20 July 2011.
24 Ibid.
25 Ibid.
26 'In Fashion', Gareth Pugh, interviewed 10 May 2010 by Alex Fury, www.SHOWstudio.com

Ballgowns:
The Rituals of Dressing Up

....

1 The absence of debutante ballgowns in this discussion is a reflection of the V&A collection's emphasis on other types of high occasion eveningwear.
2 David Sassoon and Sinty Stemp, *The Glamour of Bellville Sassoon* (London, 2008), p.130.
3 Author's interview with Roland Mouret, 2011.
4 Edwina Ehrman, 'Hardy Amies, Royal Dressmaker' in Christopher Breward (ed.), *The Englishness of English Dress* (Oxford, 2002), p.135.
5 Designs from this collection were worn by Audrey Hepburn in the film *Two for the Road*, and by Anne, Lady Tennant, Viscountess Cranborne and Lady Pamela Hicks to the coming out party of Alexandra Phillips. See David Sassoon and Sinty Stemp, *The Glamour of Bellville Sassoon* (London, 2008), p.69.
6 Email correspondence with Jill Ritblat, 19 May 2011.
7 For a useful discussion of London's couture system, see Amy de la Haye, 'Material Evidence: London Couture 1947–57' in Claire Wilcox (ed.), *The Golden Age of Couture* (V&A, 2007).
8 Email correspondence with Jill Ritblat, 19 May 2011.
9 Ibid.
10 Author's interview with Gayle Hunnicutt, 19 May 2011.
11 Email correspondence with Gnyuki Torimaru, 7 September 2011.
12 Ibid.
13 Author's interview with Gayle Hunnicutt, 19 May 2011.
14 Before serving as a Trustee of the National Gallery, Lady Heseltine was a Trustee of the Ashmolean Museum, the V&A and the Imperial War Museum. In 2001, she donated to the V&A 16 Victor Edelstein ensembles designed between 1981 and 2001.
15 Author's interview with Lady Heseltine, 20 July 2011.
16 Ibid.
17 Author's correspondence with Lady Heseltine, 18 April 2011.
18 Author's interview with Lady Heseltine, 20 July 2011.
19 Catherine Walker, *Fit for a Princess* (London, 2008), p.73.
20 Tim Graham and Tamsin Blanchard, *Dressing Diana* (London, 1998).
21 'Osman Yousefzada is the Rising Star of Fashion', *Evening Standard*, 25 March 2010.
22 Ibid.
23 Email correspondence with Nicolette Kwok, 19 July 2011.
24 Ibid.

Further Reading

Amies, Hardy
Just so Far
(London, 1954)

Beaton, Cecil
The Glass of Fashion
(London, 1954)

Beaton, Cecil
Fashion: An Anthology by Cecil Beaton
(London, 1971)

Black, Alexandra
*Dusk till Dawn: A History of the
Evening Dress*
(London, 2004)

Breward, C., Conekin, B., Cox, C., eds
The Englishness of English Dress
(Oxford, 2002)

Breward, C., Ehrman, E. and Evans, C.
*The London Look: Fashion from Street
to Catwalk*
(London, 2004)

Eastoe, Jane and Gristwood, Sarah
Fabulous Frocks
(London, 2008)

Evans, C., Menkes, S., Quinn, B.
Polhemus, T.
Hussein Chalayan
(Rotterdam, 2005)

de la Haye, Amy
*The Cutting Edge: 50 years of British
Fashion 1947–1997* (London, 1996)

Hartnell, Norman
Silver and Gold
(London, 1955)

Reeder, Jan Glier
*High Style: Masterworks from the
Brooklyn Museum Costume Collection
at the Metropolitan Museum of Art*
(New York, 2010)

Rhodes, Zandra and Knight, Anne
The Art of Zandra Rhodes
(London, 1984)

Sassoon, David and Stemp, Sinty
The Glamour of Bellville Sassoon
(London, 2008)

Torimaru, Gnyuki
Yuki
(London, 1998)

Walker, Catherine
Catherine Walker: Fit For a Princess
(London, 1998)

Watt, Judith
Ossie Clark: 1965–74 (London, 2003)

Wilcox, Claire
*The Golden Age of Couture: Paris and
London 1947–57* (London, 2007)

Acknowledgements

This book is the result of the efforts and expertise of a wide range of generous contributors. Foremost we would like to thank David Hughes for producing such wonderful images and interpreting the dresses with his unique vision. We would also like to thank Julie Brown at MAP, Simon Farrant, Ivan Ruberto and Jason Hill (retouching) at ProVision Photographic. Many thanks are due to Vincent Olivieri, Theo Politowicz and Lynda Gray for the ingenious prop designs, ably assisted by Killa Car-Ince and Barbara Wolff. We are very appreciative of the support of Glenn Benson and the team at Blythe House who facilitated the photographic shoot. In addition we extend our thanks to Coutts for their sponsorship and to all the donors and lenders of the beautiful dresses showcased within these pages.

We are grateful to Magda Keaney for her input into the project and for her wonderful introduction to the book. Thank you to all of our colleagues in the V&A's Furniture Textiles and Fashion department, particularly Christopher Wilk and Claire Wilcox for supporting the project. Thanks are also due to Liz Miller for her time and invaluable comments. We are indebted to our hard-working team of volunteers Emily Ardizzone, Ella Predota Davison, Alicia DeToro, Bryony Edwards, Matthew Greer, Rebecca Sadtler and Christine Teeling.

The V&A publishing team were incredibly responsive to our suggestion of commissioning a book on fashion as seen through the prism of a photographer's lens. Many thanks are due to Mark Eastment, Clare Davis, Kate Phillimore and Kaitlyn Whitley but most especially Anjali Bulley, whose hard work made this publication possible. We are grateful to Adam Brown for his elegant design and Denny Hemming for her editing of the text.

Oriole Cullen thanks friends and family. Sonnet Stanfill, thanks her mother, Silver Stanfill, for her characteristically insightful suggestions.

Picture Credits

Fig.1	David Hughes/ *Ponystep* magazine	Fig.25	catwalking.com
Fig.3	© Harry Benson	Fig.26	David Lake Photography Ltd
Fig.6	© Alpha Press		
Fig.7	Picture Press Ltd/Alamy		
Fig.8	Trinity Mirror/Mirrorpix/ Alamy		
Fig.9	Popperfoto/Getty Images		
Fig.10	Daniel Farson/Picture Post/Getty Images		
Fig.11	V&A Archives		
Fig.12	Getty Images		
Fig.13	Desmond O'Neill		
Fig.15	Jayne Fincher/Princess Diana Archive/Getty Images		
Fig.16	© Alpha Press		
Fig.17	Pierre Verdy/AFP/Getty Images		
Fig.18	© Edward Le Poulin/ Corbis		
Fig.19	V&A Archives		
Fig.20	Getty Images		
Fig.21	© Edward Le Poulin/ Corbis		
Fig.22	Henry Clarke/ *Vogue* © The Condé Nast Publications Ltd		
Fig.24	Tim Graham/ Getty Images